Dear Mary,

I am so expensive [proud?] of you, my second daughter.

I hope this book by Dr. Una, one of my favorite teachers & coaches, will inspire you as you see glimpses of your own journey in it...

THE FIGHT TO BECOME

Become, → Then
Be! Do! Have!

Dr. Una

Be who He says!
Do what He says!
Have what He says!

Much love,
Alise

December 25, 2024

Copyright © 2018 Dr. Una
All rights reserved.
ISBN:
978-1-963503-06-7

ACKNOWLEDGEMENTS

To my Lord Jesus who has always been there for me.

To my husband, Steve, who is my chief motivator and encourager.

To our four wonderful kids: Cheta, Chidi, Chi Chi and Esther, the joy of my life.

To my sister, Ejay, who makes me look so much better than I am.

To my brother, Obi, my everything IT guy.

To my parents, Ekene and Ego Chineme, who gave up so much to give me the life I have.

To Makeda, personal assistant extraordinaire.

To my mentors who showed me that impossible is nothing.

To you, the reader, who inspired this book.

CONTENTS

ACKNOWLEDGEMENTS 3

PROLOGUE 6

CHAPTER ONE: *A new chapter begins* 11

CHAPTER TWO: *Steve* 19

CHAPTER THREE: *Newark Beth Israel* 30

CHAPTER FOUR: *Georgia* 38

CHAPTER FIVE: *Ivy League Pediatrics* 43

CHAPTER SIX: *Two of my miracle babies* 59

CHAPTER SEVEN: *Parenting, the most overwhelming thing I have ever done.* 72

CHAPTER EIGHT: *My struggle with depression* 76

CHAPTER NINE: *My power habits* 86

CHAPTER TEN: *My most powerful life lesson* 96

CHAPTER ELEVEN: *My Superpower* 100

CHAPTER TWELVE: *My Why* 109

EPILOGUE 115

WHO IS DR. UNA? 117

HOW CAN I WORK WITH DR. UNA? 119

PROLOGUE

I have never really been a party kind of girl. Don't believe me? Well, check this out: I got married on a Tuesday in my dad's living room!

I thought about all the parties people throw to celebrate their 40th birthdays and decided I did not want a party, but I did want to give back in a big way. I dreamt up a conference, celebration of life service in church and a series of Facebook Live events to share my story. The dream was really coming alive and then I realized that my 40th birthday was too far away, and I wanted to do something now.

So, what am I doing?

I am giving back in a big way on my 39th birthday! 39 is the new 40 (that's my line and I am sticking with it).

I am writing this book to share my story because I want to inspire you. I want to let you know that you can overcome your fears, limitations, circumstances, and obstacles. I want to let you know that you can live a life of significance. I tell my life story not because my life is the standard or is better than yours, but because I have learned lessons in areas where you may not have taken classes yet.

I have learned from others and from the school of hard knocks and I would like to give you a shortcut. Why do trial and error when you can benefit from my depth of experience and extensive research?

Get ready for a roller coaster ride that has led to where I am now. I have been married for 11 years, have 4 amazing children and I have the privilege of mentoring many people and watching them become great. My husband and I own a pediatric practice called Ivy League Pediatrics and other businesses.

That might sound like a lot but trust me, by the time you are done with this book you will realize that if someone like me could become the woman I am today- you can become the person you are designed to be.

What I love to read the most are autobiographies. Why? Well, because it shows the things that great people had to go through before they made it. When I read them, I realize that if they could make it in spite of all the setbacks, disappointments and faults they had, then so can I.

The biggest lesson I have learned in the last 39 years is that you can maximize your potential and become all you are called to be but in order to do get there, you must fight! You cannot look at obstacles as problems. They are not. For you to be a victor, you have to have fought some battles and won them. For you to become a champion, you must have fought and outsmarted every roadblock in your way.

You might say, 'I knew it, success is not for me, I am not a fighting person'. I am writing this to let you know that anyone can fight. My temperament is phlegmatic which means that by nature, I will do anything to avoid conflict. By nature, I was not a fighter but I discovered that I would either learn how to fight or be content with not becoming much in life. It is as though all the forces of nature are ready to help but they will not take a step till you take a stand. A stand to reject the option of you being less than everything you can be.

At the start of my journey, I was not necessarily doing poorly. I mean I had a lot of things going right for me. However, I was not even beginning to scratch the depth of my potential. There was so much more. And you cannot touch the 'so much more' until you take a stand to fight.

Maybe that is you. Maybe you have a great job, wonderful family, you're out of debt and generally comfortable. Maybe you compare yourself to your peers and you are grateful that you are better off. That's good but is that all there is to your life? What if you could take a look at who you were designed to be, you at the age of 100 years. What do you think that you would have accomplished? I do not know the answer to that question, but I can tell you that you would not look like *this* you. My hope is that this book arouses in you a warrior mentality that will make you blast through obstacles and past circumstances to become all that you can be.

It is time to step out of your comfort zone and into the fighting ring.

Happy reading!

Dr. Una

CHAPTER ONE-
A new chapter begins

It was the 5th of October, 2004 and I was sitting in the Amsterdam Airport in Schiphol. I had a 7-hour layover between Lagos, Nigeria, and New Jersey. 7 hours would seem like a long time, but the Amsterdam airport is a thing of beauty. More than 75 duty-free stores with fairly steep discounts and great places to eat so I managed to have an amazing time. I had just completed my one-year internship after medical school. I went to the University of Nigeria which was one of the most prestigious colleges in the country. It was a very rough road. The Nigerian medical colleges use the same system as the English schools. They give as many people as possible the opportunity to get into medical school and then it is survival of the fittest. In my class, we started off with over 400 students but only about 108 ended up graduating. When I think about medical school, I think 'that was great, but I will never do that again'.

Anyway, back to Amsterdam. I was sitting in the airport and I had enough time to window shop and to think. I was going from the known to the unknown. I was going to New Jersey to take my board exams and hopefully get into a residency program to become a pediatrician. There was just so much uncertainty. What if I did not pass my exams? What if I was not able to get a residency spot? What if I got a spot but was not able to adapt to the new environment I would find myself in? Needless to say, it was an exciting and scary time.

I remember praying and asking God to help me. I remember putting everything into His hands. I do not know how to explain what happened next, other than to say that I had a knowing and this is what it was.

"If you will stay prayerful, be very generous and work hard, I will take care of you"

I figured that was simple enough and 12 years later, I can tell you it worked!

I got into NJ, and boy was it cold! My aunt laughed at me, but I had been living in year-round summers for the last 21 years, so the fall was just too much for me.

THE FIGHT TO BECOME

After settling in, it was time to get to work. I had two exams that I had to ace by the end of the year.

I had to learn how to work the Metro (I had not learned to drive but please don't tell) and made my way to the library to study for 6-9 hours every day. Because I had gone to medical school in Africa, I was an expert in tropical medicine, but all my testing was in temperate medicine. It was very hard to do. You see, studying for 6-9 hours every day is like going to the gym every morning. Some days you will feel like it, some days you won't. The difference between those that accomplish stuff and those that don't is that winners do what they need to do whether they feel like it or not. Some days I did not want to, some days I had a headache, some days I felt like I could not understand what I was reading but I just had to keep going. I felt like quitting a lot of times, but I didn't and I'm glad I didn't.

The day came when I had passed my first exam, scoring at the 95th percentile and I was the happiest girl on the planet!!!!!!!!! After months of uncertainty, this was the first sign that I was going to make it. My confidence hit the roof and I was ready to take on the next challenge.

Phase one was over and it was now time for phase 2- getting a residency spot.

I got a few interviews in New York and none in New Jersey but I really wanted to stay in New Jersey.

I remember checking my email and getting an invitation to interview at the Newark Beth Israel Medical Center Pediatric Residency program. I was elated but that happy feeling lasted for all of 3 minutes before it was replaced with some anxiety.

I was going to have to walk into a hospital bigger than any I had ever seen and impress them enough that they would offer me a position.

What if they asked me questions I could not answer?

What if I was too intimidated and I froze during the interview?

I was intimidated and a little nervous but at this stage in my life, I had learned to do it afraid. I prayed like crazy before the interview because I really needed God's help.

I started off the interview with the program director. After interviewing me and introducing me to some other faculty members, he took me over to Dr. Anyaoku to interview me. It was the most amazing interview ever. I did not know this at the beginning, but Dr. Anyaoku was an Alumni of the University of Nigeria as well! What are the odds? She did what she should to interview me as a candidate and then we talked about the medical college, transitions and all and then she gave me her contact information to stay in touch.

I left there feeling like it went very well. I excitedly told my mentor at the time about it. He asked if they offered me the position. I started to explain that that is not exactly the way things worked. They would interview all their candidates first and then go through the match and all this took at least 4 months from when my interview happened.
Well, turns out my mentor is not about that life.
'Do they ever offer people positions outside the match process?' he asked.

'Yes', I replied, and I immediately understood what he wanted me to do.

I want to say I was very bold and I called them up the next day, but I did not. I sent them an email and to my amazement, I got a response in less than an hour. I was invited back to the office and I was a offered a job contingent on passing my second exam which I was scheduled to take in December of 2004. I could not believe it but in November, *less than 6 weeks after I had come to the USA*, I had aced my first exam and had a contract in my hands.

At this point, I was on a roll. However, if you are making progress in your life, you will be challenged constantly. You will have brief periods to rest and celebrate then you must get back to the grind. How brief should this time be? I don't know, but take a hint from the fact that God in the story of creation worked for 6 days and rested for one. The key is to not rest too much. If your life feels like a holiday, you are in your comfort zone and that is the worst place you can find yourself. The comfort zone is the burial ground of great destinies and should be avoided like the plague.

THE FIGHT TO BECOME

After celebrating the first 2 victories, the next hurdle was passing my second exam, the USMLE Step 2 CS. This was not like any of the other exams I had taken because, in this one, I would actually have to see test patients, get a history, examine them and document my diagnosis and treatment plan! All this over an 8-hour period with 12 different patients. I think a written test is nerve-racking enough, but this kind of in-person test where you are literally being watched as you do your 'doctor thing' takes nerve-racking to a whole new level.

I was beginning to get the hang of a life lesson that has served me well.

Do your best, pray, and let God do the rest.

I did a lot of studying and practicing and flew out to Houston to take my exam. How did it go? It went great overall. However, in the 8 hours it took to take the exam, there were so many opportunities for discouragement and self-doubt. It is easy to start anything confidently. The challenge is keeping the confidence throughout the process, or at least not quitting when the confidence wanes. When I was done, I guessed I passed but I did feel like I had just walked out of a wrestling match.

I did some sightseeing in Houston and flew back to New Jersey.

December came and went and in January, I found out I passed my Step 2 CS! I called the residency coordinator at Newark Beth Israel to update my file and I was all set to begin my pediatric residency in June of the following year, 2005.

I learned a valuable lesson over that 3-month process. Look your fears in the face and dare them. Take action in the direction of your goals and even though you're afraid, you will make significant progress.

CHAPTER TWO
Steve

With a contract in hand and 6 months to spare before residency would start, I kicked back a little bit. I wanted to get a job to make some money on the side, but it was so hard to get my social security number. You see, I was born in San Francisco but at the time, social security numbers were not required to enroll in school, so my parents never applied. Imagine me showing up 26 years later telling them that I needed to get a social security card. They thought I was insane.

In the meantime, I did what I could. I knew how to braid hair, so I did that ('Oh my goodness, as a doctor you did that???' Yes, I did). I also did some direct selling with Mary Kay. I did not make a killing, but I made enough to be somewhat self-sufficient.

I did not have a large social circle at the time, so I had to talk to a lot of strangers. At that time, I was still painfully shy. I was scared to talk to people one on one and I was very afraid of rejection. So, every day, I got up and did something I absolutely hated. Now that I look back on it, I am grateful. I did not make a whole lot from it financially but that was a time where I worked on my people skills daily. Today I am in a position where I am comfortable talking to thousands of patients and their families every year. I have spoken on stages to hundreds of people at a time and I even host a weekly facebook show called the Legacy Parent Show. Like many of you who may be reading this book, I was introverted and shy, but I truly wanted to be a people person. I wanted to be able to talk freely, help people and genuinely have fun with people. It's been a few years since I went door to door to get new clients but now I can say I have made that transition. I am able to talk freely, help people and genuinely have fun with them. Am I still working on this? Absolutely, but I am nowhere near where I used to be. Most times, when I share this part of my story, people find it hard to reconcile the old me and the new me and that can be you too. I am still an introvert at heart, but I call myself an extroverted introvert.

THE FIGHT TO BECOME

I kept working and using my time the best way I knew how. That December, I got introduced to Steve. Actually, that is really pushing it. Someone told me about him. Steve was an entrepreneur and pastor of a campus fellowship in Nigeria at the time. I was going to go to Nigeria in April prior to starting residency so I figured I would meet him then.

In April, I went to Port-Harcourt, Nigeria and had a blast. My parents were very happy to see me and of course very proud of me. Like a lot of parents in their generation, they said nothing to me about how proud they were but bragged non-stop whenever they were talking to their friends. That had to do, at least I still got to hear it.

On that same trip, I finally met him. The first thing that drew me to him was that he was extremely confident and was not intimidated by the fact that I was a doctor or anything of the sort. At the time, he did not have much, but he was a visionary and knew where he was going. To top it off, he was and still is a very handsome man and a power dresser. These and the fact that he dotted on me made this deal a sealed deal. He was the one.

I consider myself a different kind of gal. I am very calculative and deliberate. As a single person, when I thought of marriage, I thought of it as a strategic merger of lives, with all the romance and roses and sweet talk being what they should be- the icing on the cake. If someone came to tell me about someone they were thinking of getting married to, I would literally dig and ask them questions to get a pros and cons list. It's just the way my mind works.

My mom quickly caught on and was all for it. You may not know much about the Nigerian culture, but I'll tell you this. ALL parents want their kids married and churning out grandchildren as quickly and often as possible. That's all I'm going to say about that.

Anyway, a year later we got married and it has been such a great ride. We have been married for 11 years and we are more in love than ever. Are we perfect? Absolutely not! However, we are aware that we are two people with great hearts sprinkled with some faults who have decided that with God's help we will work.

The movie industry has led us to believe that when you find the right one, you will live happily ever after, but every married person knows that is not true. Finding the right person is very important but if you find the right person and still refuse to do the work, you will be living in hell on earth.

Marriage is work, hard work, but it is work that pays off. If you will play marriage by the rules, you will create your own heaven on earth. My husband describes a perfect marriage this way:

A woman 100% focused on the happiness of her husband and a man focused 100% on the happiness of his wife.

My marriage is one of the most valuable things to me. This story demonstrates one of the benefits of a stable, healthy marriage.

There is a story about a contest in Canada for the strongest ox. The winning ox could pull 8,000 pounds and the runner-up pulled just a little less than that. The owners of the oxen wanted to know how much the two oxen could pull together. Most observers placed a bet around 16,000 pounds. Some bet a little more, some a little less. When they actually put the two oxen in front of the weights, they pulled over 26,000 pounds!

That is true synergy: the whole is greater than the sum of its parts. That is why team playing is so much more effective.

I believe that our lives as individuals get turbo charged after we get married. It is so weird that opposites attract. Usually, we choose people who are strong where we are weak and weak where we are strong. That is perfect because when we become one in the context of marriage, the strengths cancel out the weaknesses.

If you are married, do the hard work, it has a great pay off.

I had watched enough movies to know that after the wedding, the next thing that should happen is that we should live happily ever after. Within the first 2 weeks, it became apparent that the happily ever after happens after a whole lot of work has been done on the marriage not before. We did not have drawn out fights or yelling matches or anything like that but we were definitely not one. You see, as a person of faith, I believed the Bible before understanding what it said.

The scriptures say,

"And the two shall become one flesh".

I thought that meant after the wedding but it actually talks about a process.

The more time you spend together, the more you communicate with the intent to understand, the more you resolve the inevitable conflict, the more one you will become and the more of a happily ever after you will experience.

Marriage is designed to work like wine. It should get better with age.

It is not the warm and fuzzy lovey feelings that make a marriage work, it is commitment and work. The warm, fuzzy, lovey feelings are the icing on the cake.

Don't be thrown off by conflict in your marriage. You have had conflict with everyone else in your life- your parents, your siblings, your friends, your roommates, your professors, some of us have even been super mad at God whom we have never seen. Your relationship with your spouse will be no different. You will have conflict.

Marriages that fail and those that thrive have conflict in common. The question becomes, how skilled are the husband and the wife at conflict resolution.

In my home, we have learned to resolve conflict quickly. We recognize that if we have an issue, that is exactly what it is, an issue. So we stand together and fight the issue, not one another. It has served us well and we have a great relationship and a peaceful home.

One of the major causes of divorce worldwide is money problems. As a young couple, we made a decision that we would be content with where we were financially, and we would only upgrade as our finances upgraded.

When we first started off, we were living in a cheap apartment in Irvington, NJ. It was not in a nice part of town, nor was it very comfortable, but it was not unsafe. It was a one-bedroom apartment that we made home—our home. Could we afford it? Yes. We were not under any pressure to pay the rent or our utilities.

THE FIGHT TO BECOME

For the most part, we shared one car, a 10-year-old Toyota Camry, (that is, until we got suckered into leasing a Nissan Altima, but that is a story for another day). It was not a flashy car or a car you would think that a doctor should drive but it was reliable. It took us anywhere we needed to go. I remember going to work one day and one of my attendings was encouraging me to buy a Mercedes G class, an $85,000 car. I looked at him like he had lost his mind. He kept going and on about how it was an amazing car. Now if I wanted it bad enough I could have made the payments work but as a resident, I was making $42,000 a year. If I threw every single penny of my paycheck at it for 2 years, I would not even have finished paying off the car. In my book, even though I might have been able to make the payments, I definitely could not 'afford' the car.

In the beginning, if we wanted to take all the debt we could afford to, we could have lived in a nicer place and bought a brand new car. However, we chose to grow slowly but surely rather than jumping the gun and creating unnecessary financial pressure.

As our income increased, we were able to afford the finer things. We grew into affording bigger apartments and ultimately our own home. From 10-year-old cars to brand new cars. This took away a lot of financial stress because we just did not do things we could not afford to do.

To my single friends, lose the Hollywood mindset. If what you see in the movies is true, the divorce rate in the US would not be 50% with the same actors that portrayed the stories leading the way to the divorce courts.

The advice I will give you in this book is to choose wisely. The choice of who to marry is not a casual one and should be taken very seriously.
Your choice is yours, but first, you make your choice, and then your choice will make you.

Read about marriage from people with a proven track record, and also run your decision by people who are successful at marriage, care about you and will tell you the truth.

Steve is the best thing other than Jesus that has happened to me. In addition to all the other things that an awesome husband does, he is also my number one mentor. You see, the person I am today is a major upgrade from the young woman he married 11 years ago. He has always inspired me, supported me, held me accountable and cheered me on. I learned from him how to be a dreamer and how to grind until those dreams become a reality. There are so many things I have accomplished only because of him. One day a few years ago, we had started a project I never thought of doing and I looked at him and told him something that is so true:

'Doing life with you is like hanging on the outside of an 18-wheeler while you are in the driver's seat racing down the interstate at 100 miles per hour'.

He does life in the fast lane. Not in a reckless way but with the understanding that you only live life once and you must create a legacy with it. He taught me that I won't always have the strength that I have now, I won't always have the same opportunities I have now, and every day that passes is a day I can never get back.

From him, I learned to be intentional about life. Like Brian Tracy said, this is not a rehearsal, it is the only life we will get to live.

CHAPTER THREE
Newark Beth Israel

Residency was a brutal three years. 80-hour work weeks with little pay and little appreciation. I was grateful I had the opportunity and I knew that the process had an expiration date. If you want to be a doctor because you watched House or Grey's Anatomy, don't do it. It is not related to reality at all.

It was during my residency training that I chose to adopt the attitude of gratitude. I learned to always see the glass as half full as opposed to half empty. Rather than gripe and complain like everyone else, I would look for the things in that situation to be grateful to God for. I could be thankful:

- That I got accepted into a program because there were people better than me that did not get a spot.

THE FIGHT TO BECOME

- That I was healthy enough to go through the program because there were people that had to drop out because of health problems.
- That I had a supportive family.

And the list would go on and on and on.

It worked though. I remember a 3rd-year resident talking to me when I was an intern and asking, 'How do you do it? You actually seem to be enjoying residency!"

Residency is one of the hardest things I have ever done. I am glad I went through it but I will never do it again! It was a whole world of uncertainty. On my first day, I was overjoyed and terrified at the same time. It was an exciting new world. I had the privilege of working directly with many unbelievably talented attendings. As an intern, I reported to the 2nd year, 3rd year residents and my attendings. I was as green as could be. I did not know how the attendings wanted the patients to be discussed or how to do a lot of the procedures that needed to be done. I didn't even know the layout of the pediatric unit. I learned very quickly how to learn what I did not know. I learned how to take corrections without feeling like a dummy because I needed to be corrected every day. That was not bad because I was in a training program, but things like that over time can get to you and shake your confidence.

After a few weeks, I got used to the system and started doing my job more confidently. The funny thing though is that all our rotations were broken into 4-week blocks. As soon as you get used to one block and feel like you will make it, you get thrown into a whole new thing.

I went from outpatient pediatrics with mostly healthy kids who were there for a checkup, to the Neonatal Intensive care unit (NICU) with 1 lb babies born at 24 weeks fighting for their lives, to the Pediatric inpatient unit with sickle cell patients in crisis, round and round I went, just like a merry-go-round, but not as fun!

There were also so many procedures to learn. How to start IV lines, draw blood, catheterize babies to get urine, do spinal taps, intubate patients, fix dislocated joints, perform CPR on unconscious patients, it was endless! One by one, I began to master these and ultimately, I did feel a bit like a procedure queen.

THE FIGHT TO BECOME

In addition to this, the hours were brutal. 24-hour calls that usually turned into 30-hour calls with a few cat naps if you were exceptionally lucky. It was really hard during the winter months because I would leave my house when it was dark and get back after it was dark. I would sometimes go for days and the only sunlight I would see was when I was fortunate enough to peak out of a patient's room window during rounds.

To survive, I had to learn to work with all kinds of people. There were lazy colleagues who intended to do the least amount of work possible, so others had to pick their slack. I learned to pretend I did not know what they were trying to do and drag them along to do the work with me. There were colleagues who would try to take credit for the work that you did. I maintained my cool when they did that because in the end they would always get found out. No need to act the fool or wreck the rest of my day because of them. There were colleagues that seemed to be paralyzed by fear and I learned to be their number one cheerleader till they got to the place of confidence. There were the super smart ones with amazing work ethics and I learned to keep them close and copy them.

It was constantly challenging but that is the nature of the beast. It was a training program, after all.

It was sometimes a very hostile environment. I remember being on call in the NICU one night. Now, this was a 70-bed NICU with a lot of really sick premature babies. You didn't do this call hoping to catch a break at all because it was always so busy. The very premature babies were usually dependent on breathing machines and they were connected to these by breathing tubes. The sickest baby in the unit that night was a baby born at 24 weeks that weighed 500 grams. She literally weighed half a pound!

Well, in the early hours of the morning, probably by 2 am, her breathing tube got disconnected from her airways. A code was called and there was chaos everywhere. Intubating a 30-week 2 pound baby can sometimes be a challenge, but this was expected to be quite the feat. I was closest to the room where the child was, so I raced in to try to put the tube back in. I was a second-year resident, so I had done a fair number of intubations and I was confident I could get it in. The nurse in charge of the baby yelled at the top of her lungs, 'Someone get me a real doctor in here'.

THE FIGHT TO BECOME

I did not bother responding verbally or emotionally, I just continued what I was doing. I placed the half pound baby in position and got to work.

'Laryngoscope'. The respiratory therapist at my side handed it to me.

I inserted it and could see extremely tiny airways.

'Endotracheal tube'. Again, the respiratory therapist handed it to me.

'Cricoid pressure please'. He applied pressure while I inserted the tube.

At this time, the supervising neonatologist on call had come to the bedside but chose to allow me to finish the procedure. Immediately after I was done, the respiratory therapist tested to confirm the tube was in the right place. He used a cool gadget called a colorimeter. When attached to the end of a properly placed tube, the CO_2 produced with exhalation causes it to turn from purple to yellow. As soon as he connected the tube to the colorimeter it turned yellow!!! I stopped holding my breath and thanked God that it went it in one try.

There was excitement in the room. The respiratory therapist and the supervising attending both patted me on the back. 'Good job', they said. 'Thank you', I heard from behind me. It was said very softly so I turned to see who had said that. It was the nurse, the same one that had asked for a 'real doctor'. I smiled at her and walked away.

There is something I hear my husband say all the time:

'Competence knows no prejudice'.

Let the haters hate. When people say mean things to you, don't take it personally. It is most likely an overflow of the frustrations they have in their own lives and they are just trying to transfer it to you. Your job is to become more competent until you can do whatever it is you do with excellence.

It was not all stress though. I did have a lot of fun times in residency. We had potlucks, celebrated birthdays, attended weddings and baby showers, shared holidays together and even had a few retreats. I made lots of friends, many of whom I am still friends with today. Overall, it was a great experience. I am actually smiling as I type this.

Much as I enjoyed it, I also looked forward to its end. On August 8th, 2008 after 3 grueling years of training, I became a pediatrician. I was so grateful and amazed at the journey I had taken.

The end of a chapter is the sure sign that a new one is about to open. This is usually exciting, but it is almost always followed by the same uncertainty that always comes with a new phase.

Well, residency was over, and it was now time to go into the real world.

CHAPTER FOUR
Georgia

My husband and I knew that we wanted to move to Georgia. I applied for a job in Stockbridge while I was still a resident and got invited for an interview.

We both came to Georgia for the interview and fell more in love with Georgia. At the end of the interview, my potential boss and I decided we would be a good fit so I accepted the offer. Once I finished my last shift as a resident, we packed up our things and moved to the South.

We were very happy about the move and quickly settled in. I started my job at Southside Pediatrics in Stockbridge, GA. The Saturday after we drove into Atlanta, something wonderful happened. We met with Mr. Dominic, a man we had heard of through a mutual acquaintance and we had a prayer meeting that lasted for an hour. This meeting has grown and morphed into what is now Dominion City Church, Norcross, GA.

THE FIGHT TO BECOME

Why did we start it as soon as we moved to Georgia? Only one reason, Steve. Like I said earlier, with him, I feel like I am on the outside of an 18-wheeler hanging on for dear life while he is driving down the interstate at 150 miles an hour. He believes in acting quickly and that is truly one of the secrets of the high-level productivity in our lives.

Over the years, we have had the privilege of serving people, helping them build a relationship with God and to find and walk in their purpose. We have seen lives transformed in every way imaginable- families restored, businesses started, people neck deep in debt becoming debt free and delinquents and misfits becoming responsible members of society. This gives us more joy than anything else we do.

My philosophy of life is that there has got to be more to life than doing well in school, getting a great job, having a wonderful family, raising children, enjoying your golden years and then dying.

As a person of faith, I am a firm believer that God is real, and the afterlife is real. I believe I will be rewarded based on what I do here to help others find and live out their purpose in life.

Being involved in starting the church, leading worship (yes, I sing), administration and mentoring others not just spiritually but in all aspects of their lives has given my life a sense of purpose. I don't think there is anything more rewarding than watching lives go from going nowhere to blossoming.

In the process of doing all of that, I had to stretch and grow significantly. I learned how to lead people, I learned how to speak on stage, how to resolve conflict between people, and I learned patience (and boy, did I need a lot of that!). These skills have served me well, not only in ministry but in every aspect of my life.

Southside Pediatrics was also a training ground for me. I worked there as a solo practitioner and did my very best there. I did more than I was required to and truly acted as a practice owner and not an employee. I did what I could to retain the current patients and developed and implemented different ways to bring new patients in. When I was doing that, I had no idea that one day I would own my own practice.

THE FIGHT TO BECOME

You see, I learned a principle from Brian Tracy and that is this- you work for yourself no matter who writes your check. I work for Dr. Una Inc. and I must work at all times to improve the value of that company.

I see people who do sloppy work because it is someone else's and dream of owning their own company. What they do not realize is that the way you act in someone else's business is ultimately the way you will act in yours. If you have not been able to discipline yourself to go to work on time at someone else's office, you will also go late when you own your own practice. The worst part is that the law of Karma will also make sure that when you hire staff it will a bunch of people just like you were at your boss's organization. Yikes!

I was so valuable to the organization I worked with that when my contract was over and I had to leave because we were relocating, he told me I might as well start my own practice. Now, at this time, I was pregnant with baby #2. I objected, citing the fact that I did not have enough experience, but he made it clear that I was doing most of the things a practice owner would do anyway. He also made himself available for any questions I would have along the way.

DR. UNA

That leads us to the next chapter, Ivy League Pediatrics.

CHAPTER FIVE
Ivy League Pediatrics

It was the 30th of March, 2010. My husband and I were sitting in Dr. Desai' office having a defining moment. We had just signed the lease for our new pediatric practice- Ivy League Pediatrics. It had taken us three months from when we decided to go for it to get to this point. We were excited and nervous, but we were willing to trust God and do the hard work to make our dream a reality.

How did we get here?

My husband and I used to take a lot of long walks in the evenings in the early years of our marriage. We would dream of owning our own businesses. To us, it was a thing that would happen in the distant future, little did we know that in less than a year it would be a reality.

I had a one-year contract at my first job in Georgia, but we were going to have to move from Stockbridge because the church we planted was in Norcross, almost an hour away. My then boss, after realizing I was going to move had encouraged me to start my own practice. I was just a year out of my pediatric residency program and I definitely did not think I had what it took to step out on my own.

2 months later, my mentor met with my husband and I and told us it was time to start our own business. He inspired us and prayed for us and left. That is the beautiful thing about mentors, they push you beyond the imaginary limits you place on yourself.

We did not have any capital to start but we started doing what we could. I remember hours and hours of research. We researched over 150 practices all over the country- studying how their offices were set up, what kind of services they offered, what they did to get 5-star reviews and what got them 1-star reviews. We got a real estate agent and started looking at possible locations.
   It seemed like an insurmountable task, but we did not stop, and then the miracles started happening.

We found an office in move in condition in Lawrenceville. It was in perfect shape and did not even need a new coat of paint, and all this at a third of the price of the other offices we looked at. That was a miracle in itself! You see, I personally do not like to look at construction sites. I like finished buildings, just my preference.

I remember going to look at the very first building. My real estate agent was so ecstatic about the place. It was close to Gwinnett Medical Center in Duluth, a renowned specialist's office, and a huge surgery practice, so it had a lot of foot traffic. She went on and on about the place and eventually got me excited about it too. Now, when I asked how much the rent would be, her first question back was, "are you sitting down?" When I said I was, she went on tell to tell me it was $3200/month. $3200/month!!!!!! I could not really wrap my head around it but I figured I would go and look at the place.

I still remember that day like it was yesterday. My husband was out of town, so I left my one-month-old baby at home and drove for a whole hour from Stockbridge to Duluth. I got there and looked at the outside and immediately fell in love. It was impressive. The $3200 started to look like a price that must be paid.

The real estate agent then unlocked the doors, walked in and still looked impressed. I walked in and I suddenly became very confused.

'This is an unfinished building!', I exclaimed. 'Yes, it is. It is called a vanilla shell. It is the best kind of office space because you can build it into exactly what you want'. I was still confused. Did she mean that I was going to spend tens of thousands of dollars building out a space that did not even belong to me?

'The best part', she went on to say, 'is that the owner of the building is an architect, so you can have him draw out the plan for the build-out'. I decided to play along and went upstairs to see him. He welcomed me into his office and showed me a few projects he had worked in the past. After that, he told me that it would cost me roughly $72/sq ft to build out the office space and that came to about $100,000!!!!! I smiled and thanked him for his time and left. I wondered if our dream would ever become a reality. On my one-hour drive back home, I prayed a silent prayer,

"Lord, you own the whole earth and everything and everyone in it. I need an office space for Ivy League

Pediatrics that was previously owned by a medical practice so it is already built out."

Starting a practice is complicated enough and I just refused to learn how to build out buildings at the same time.

It did not happen immediately but ultimately, we found a beautiful fully finished office which became our first home- 603 Old Norcross Rd, Suite B, Lawrenceville, GA.

Next, we needed an EHR (electronic medical record). I called a few companies and did some demos. They seemed pretty nice until I found out how much they cost. The one I was leaning towards the most cost $30,000 upfront and then a monthly fee of about $200/month!!!!!!! It may as well have been a million dollars because I did not have that kind of money to pay for it.

2 days before I found this out, I had just found a new pediatrician for my daughter because we had moved. So, I called her up and asked her how much she paid for her EHR. 'The one I use is free', she said. There was an awkward moment of silence. She obviously did not

understand what I asked. So I attempted to clarify my question. 'I mean the EHR you use in your office. I am starting a practice and I just wanted to get an idea of how much you pay for yours', I said.

'The one I use is free', she said again. I was silent again. I could not believe what I was hearing. 'It's free and it is very easy to sign up for. It is as easy as creating a new yahoo account, takes less than 5 minutes', she continued. She gave me the information for the company, Practice Fusion, and lo and behold, in 5 minutes my practice as all set up!

I ran out of my room and got my husband. 'You will not believe what just happened to me!' I said. 'What happened?', he replied. I went on to tell him the whole story and we rejoiced like two little kids. You can't blame us. We went from needing a $30,000 down payment for a medical record system to having a medical record system for free with no strings attached in one evening. All in one evening!

Now we needed the capital to get the business going, so I starting applying for loans. I figured I could get $25,000 to get it off the ground. Everyone said no.

THE FIGHT TO BECOME

Everyone! Some said I was not creditworthy. I wasn't. I mean, I had only had a social security number for 3 years so there was no history really. Others said they don't finance 'small' loans like the meager $25,000 I was asking for.

Why did I only want that amount? Well, because I did not want to have a lot of debt going in. I decided I would get a job while building the practice that could take care of some of the bills until Ivy (that is what we call her, she is like one of our children) could take care of her bills herself.

When I saw that I would not be getting a loan, I had no idea what to do. Not having that option was not something I had anticipated. I did what I could which was pray and keep looking. One morning, I suddenly had an idea to call Dr. Dada, one of the pediatricians that trained me in New Jersey and ask her for $10,000.

I told my husband about it and he was all for it. 'Call her today', he said.

I would like to say I called her that day but I did not.

You see, asking people for things was very far out of my comfort zone.

I thought all kinds of things:

'She will say no and the relationship you have with her will be ruined'.

'She doesn't have an extra $10,000 just laying around to give you'.

'You are going to look like a fool'.

'That idea is just stupid'.

Finally, after about 2 weeks, I called her. I was nervous about the potential outcome of the conversation. After a little small talk, I got down to business. My attitude was, I'd just do it. The worst thing that could happen would be I'd have the same amount of money that I started off with.

'Steve and I have decided to open our own practice', I said. 'That is great! I am so happy to hear that', she replied.'I am calling because I am working on raising the funds I need to get this off the ground and I was wondering if you could lend me $10,000 and I'll pay back as soon as I can'. 'Sure, I can have the check mailed out to you tomorrow', she casually answered. What? It was that simple. I was stressing myself out for nothing.

THE FIGHT TO BECOME

I thanked her to the point that she probably got embarrassed.

$10,000 does not seem like much but that was all the capital I had to start Ivy League Pediatrics and it worked.

How did we make it work? We ran a lean operation and made it better as we went.

Our initial office was a little less than 1500 sq. ft and the rent was under $2000/month. We looked for deals everywhere. We found offices that were closing or downsizing and rather than pay for storage, they were willing to give us their office equipment for pennies on the dollar. My husband and I wore all the hats. All of them! We opened, we closed. We cleaned the office, answered the phones, went to Ob/Gyns and daycares to market the practice. I answered the phone to set up appointments, did the patient's vitals when they came, examined them and gave the shots myself.

We worked hard and God blessed our effort. Within 6 months, Ivy was able to pay its own bills (excluding my salary which I did not draw for the first 9 months).

As time went on and more clients came, we hired staff, moved to a bigger office, redid our website and ultimately became who we are today.

We applied the same principle we had used in our personal finances which had served us well. We started from where we were and committed to the process of continual improvement.

I am so honored by the privilege I have to partner with parents to take care of their kids. My dream has always been to bring expert medical care with a personable touch. I want the practice to run on time while remaining warm and friendly. We have made significant strides and I am proud of what we have built, however constant improvement is our motto and we keep at it.

Moral of the story? Until you make a decision to accomplish something and you start taking steps in that direction, you will never know what is possible. You may say you are scared but like I read many years ago, the only difference between a person who is courageous and another who is not is that someone is not telling the truth. Most wildly successful people do it afraid.

Fortune truly does favor the bold.

This all happened 8 years ago but today, Ivy League Pediatrics is a multi-site thriving medical practice. I have had to learn so many lessons along the way and here are some of them.

- How to be a salesperson- I was naive to think that if I hang the shingle people would come. How deceived I was. We started the practice and then crickets. The fancy phones were not ringing and no one was walking through the doors. My husband and I had to hit the streets and do what needed to be done online. We went to daycare centers, churches, apartment complexes and fairs to get the name out there.

- How to be a leader- You can hire people but that does not make you a leader. One of the hallmarks of a leader is the ability to create and manage a winning team. I remember reading a book and the author said the #1 job of a CEO is to hire and fire. I thought he must have lost his mind. Surely there is so much more to being a CEO than that. Well, as soon as I hired my first staff, I found out that author was right and silently apologized. I had to learn the very hard way that hiring, leading and dehiring is one of the key skills I must develop. I am still on my way, but I can say I am light years better. I am proud of the team I have.

- How to develop a thick skin- You will need this for 2 reasons. One is that once you become a business owner, your mistakes will be unforgivable genuine as they may be. You will be criticized, and people will take to social media to lash out. Complaints are not entirely bad. It shows you points for improvement. In Ivy League Pediatrics, we convert complaints into projects and go to work to eliminate them. It may not be immediate, but we work on it. It does not change the fact that being called out online or to your face hurts. I had to learn to not let it hurt more than it needs to but to always use it to get better. The second reason is that you will get criticized and slammed online even if you do a great job. However, if you do a good job, you will have more grateful clients than those that criticize, always remember that. You will get depressed and quit if you do not keep that in perspective. For me, I have to focus on the 15-20 parents every day that are able to get same day appointments and avoid a 2 hour wait in the ED, the patients who we are able to get in and out of the office in under an hour which we do 95% of the time, and the kids who we serve in such a personable way that they are excited to come see us when they are sick. So, I remember the good and convert my weaknesses to projects, so that I can keep getting better.

- How to build a company culture- Now this took me a few years to figure out. Every company has a culture and it usually comes out of the core values of the visionary of the company. I'll give you one example. I believe the place of work is a place of work, so people should work all the time they are at work. If you think it is not that serious, I should inform you that statistics prove that the average employees only work 2 hours and 53 minutes of the 8-hour work day costing companies billions of dollars every year. As an employer, you do your staff a great disservice if you do not train them to up their level of productivity as this will rob them professionally and personally. I teach my staff the 48/12 principle that I learned from Brian Tracy. This is one of the habits of very successful people. Every hour is made up of 60 minutes. You put your head down and work for 48 minutes nonstop. No chatting with coworkers, coffee breaks, pee breaks, idling at all. You come up for air for 12 minutes and then go back to it. We are at work to wow our patients and their families. Until all tasks are complete, there is no time to idle. This is a culture that is ingrained in Ivy League Pediatrics. However, to this day, I go to work or train and delegate in order to preserve that culture. The second I take my eyes off it, it starts to fade. When new staff come on board, we train them and hold them accountable to this until it becomes a habit. In your company or family, this is one of the things you will have to consistently and aggressively preserve, or the culture will only be yours and not that of the whole company.

- How to keep the main thing the main thing- My business exists to serve kids and their families. It is not to make money, it is not to make a name. If service is not the reason for your business, chances are you will be miserable, you may quit and surely will not do what it takes to continually improve your business. As far as my business goes, my patients are my why and I do all I can to stay on course.

- How to never quit- We live in a generation when quitting is the easiest thing ever. In business, there will be a thousand reasons not to go on. There will be fiercer competition, high staff turnover, cash flow problems, a series of negative reviews, there is no end to the problems you will face. To compound this even further, there is the shiny object syndrome. A new opportunity comes along that seems easier and you just feel like 'escaping' to that new business so you can be rid of all the current problems. The only issue with that is that every business has storms. Notice I said storms, not a storm. There will be a series of them you will experience, sometimes even back to back. Last year, for instance, I had 4 staff on maternity leave and two quit in a 3-month period. My office at the time was not big enough to lose 7 staff at the same time without it having a significant impact on the business. Those were interesting times, but we went through the storm and came out stronger. I wish that was an isolated incident but the path to success is littered with trials, which is why those who go through them are called champions.

These lessons have served me well, but I am still aggressively learning. So far, I am proud of what we have built. We have been voted Best of Gwinnett for the last three years: 2015, 2016 and 2017. However, what makes us most proud are the parents and their kids who choose Ivy League Pediatrics as their tribe.

CHAPTER SIX
Two of my miracle babies

Life is not a mountaintop experience. It is mountains and valleys and mountains and valleys. To have and enjoy a great life you will have to learn how to weather the valleys.

Don't wish for there to be no storms. The only way to avoid storms is to die (please don't die)!

With the birth of all 4 of my children, there were storms. All 4! In this chapter, I will share the story of the birth of my first two children. Maybe you are pregnant or going to have kids and you are either afraid or have been given a difficult diagnosis. This is just for you.

2 days after I had Cheta, my first child, I wrote a beautiful piece describing in relatively few words what happened, and I will love to share that with you.

DR. UNA

The story of Cheta, written 04/03/2008

We are very excited about the arrival of our daughter Chetachukwu, and we know that you are happy for us too. The truth though is that you will never quite understand our joy except you know the conditions of her birth. I had a wonderful pregnancy, no morning sickness, reflux, swollen feet or anything of the sort. However, a call that I got on the day after Thanksgiving 2007 when I was about 21 weeks along was to change my story.

Cheta was found to have a congenital diaphragmatic hernia, which is a hole in the diaphragm (the muscle that separates the chest from the abdomen). As a result of this defect, part of her liver was in her chest. In addition to this, she had a significant quantity of fluid in the sac around her heart. The real problem was that between the liver and the additional fluid, there was not much space left in her chest for her lungs to grow. The prognosis was pretty bad at best because she was diagnosed at a critical period of rapid lung development. She would need surgery in the first week of life and would definitely need to be on life support ranging from a regular respirator to ECMO, which is like a heart and lung bypass machine. They tried to be encouraging, but they did not downplay the fact that her condition would be critical and despite their efforts, she may not survive.

My OBGYN promptly referred us to a maternal-fetal specialist who on evaluation decided that the best place for me to receive my care would be at the Children's Hospital of Philadelphia. We were told we could opt for an abortion, the rationale being that her chances of survival were slim and even if she did make it, she would have a very complicated course. When we declined, a plan of care was developed which involved frequent follow-up visits at CHOP, which was a good 2-hour drive away, and weekly ultrasounds. The pregnancy continued with no additional complications.

At 36 weeks, I had to relocate to Philadelphia because my doctors did not want me to go into labor so far away in New Jersey. The delivery needed to occur in very controlled settings. I thought that was particularly disruptive, but I had to do what was best for Cheta. I was told that if I did not go into labor on my own they would induce me at 39 weeks. When I got there though, on further evaluation they decided the best thing would be to have her by a C-section so they could drain the fluid around her heart first and then deliver her.

In the midst of all this, there was a serious mind battle going on. My husband and I are both Christians and have experienced God's healing power personally. I had to trust God for a favorable outcome for Cheta even though all the medical knowledge in my head was fighting against all I believed in. It is traditional for Christians to believe that God heals and antagonize their doctors. Our belief is that the devil steals, kills and destroys every way he can and that God provides, saves and heals every way He can. We believe that it is God that is behind the advances in medical science and so we embrace rather than reject them. What we do not believe is that in any circumstance the doctor's word is the final say. Thank God that His word is the final authority.

Throughout the pregnancy, we continued to speak God's Word over Cheta, declaring that she was healed, that she would live and not die. We trusted that God's healing hand would make her perfect. We did everything that we knew to do according to God's principles but on the outside, it seemed like nothing was changing. The good thing is that God's word had an answer for that too. It says, "Having done all to stand, stand therefore". So that is what we did. Every week the ultrasounds looked the same and the assessment by the doctors became more and more concerning but we just stood and trusted God for a miracle. Even though we had every reason to worry, we couldn't because we had that inner peace that assured us that all was well.

I had a C-section on the 1st of April in an operating room with more than 10 physicians including Obstetricians, Anesthesiologists, Pediatric Surgeons, and Neonatologists. Cheta had the fluid around her heart drained first, and then she was delivered. She cried at birth, which no one really expected her to do because of how tiny her lungs had looked on the ultrasound. The team meant business though and she was whisked away so fast that all my husband could see was her back for all of 2 seconds. She was immediately hooked up to a breathing machine and had catheters put in every spot they could find. After the initial resuscitation, she was taken to the Intensive Care Unit. She continued to be pretty unstable and within hours of her birth the surgeon came back and said they would have to take her to the Operating Room immediately. I could understand the risk that carried. First of all, taking a newborn to the OR on the day of birth is risky, how much more an unstable one!!!!!!! Well, this is where the manifestation of the miracle of it all began.

The surgeon and anesthesiologist warned us that her critical condition made a negative outcome much more likely. We knew what we believed God for so my husband paced the hallways releasing God's creative words over the situation. She went to the operating room, her liver was pushed back into her abdomen and the defect in her diaphragm was repaired. She was completely stable after that and everyone was shocked. The lungs that everyone expected would be a big problem were working so well that even though she was on a breathing machine, they were forced to place her on the lowest settings. By the 2nd day of life, she was taken off the breathing machine and on the 3rd day she started feeding!!!!!!!!!!!!! This was very shocking for everyone because they thought that she would need to be on the breathing machine for months and even with that they were not sure the amount of lung tissue that she had was usable. Eating??? That was definitely out of the question. She surely was not supposed to be doing that. It was uphill from then onwards. It was very funny to hear her doctors and nurses talk about her. They would say things like," I think everyone except your daughter realizes that she is sick", "She has broken every record that we have", "Whatever you believe in surely works because she is a miracle".

Naturally speaking, we shouldn't have a daughter to our name and even if we did we should be with her in the Intensive Care Unit watching her battle daily for her life. We are grateful to God for what He did in her. My doctors have no explanation for how she just got better; they also had to conclude that she is a miracle.

Now that you know, you will understand why we are ecstatic!!!!!!!!!!!! It is not a coincidence that her name is Chetachukwu, which means, "Remember God and His mighty works". Cheta is the child we could have lost or that could have gone through months of illness with long-term complications. Instead, God has given her to us, completely whole, 7lbs 1 oz, 50cm long and absolutely gorgeous. Thank God with us.

Praise God!!!! That was the most faith-building journey I had been through.

The question you may be asking is, 'How did you react when you first got the news?' 'How did you manage to keep your cool all those months'?

I still remember the moment when I got the call from my Ob/Gyn. It was Black Friday 2007. I had a wonderful Thanksgiving Day with my friends the day before and I was just relaxing on my bed. Then the phone rang and my doctor broke the news. As she did, something subtle but potentially dangerous happened. Every pregnant woman has a picture of the end on the inside of her. Her holding the baby, the baby in the crib in the nursery, her giving the baby a bath and so forth. Most pregnant women have in their mind an image of a completely normal baby. As the doctor was telling me what was going on, the picture in my mind got switched. I immediately saw a picture of me sitting in the ICU with my daughter with tubes and machine connected to her tiny body and her fighting for her life.

I did not expect the news. I did not know what I was going to do but there is one thing I just knew.

THE FIGHT TO BECOME

I could not accept that picture.

I immediately said out loud- My daughter is completely whole from the crown of her head to the soles of her feet in the name of Jesus. As soon as I declared that, I willfully replaced the picture of both of us in the hospital with the picture of a perfectly healthy baby like I had in the beginning.

That was the first lesson I learned. In the face of trials and difficult times, don't accept the wrong picture and don't keep quiet. Say what you believe.

Immediately after that, I called my husband who was in Nigeria at the time and told him what was going on.

Anyone who has met my husband knows that he is a quiet person who is very easy to get along with, but I will tell you, he turns into a lion in the face of opposition. As soon as I told him what the doctor said, he said 'Go back to bed, our daughter will be just fine'. I was confident that everything would be fine even though I had no idea how. I also talked to Yaminah, my dear friend and fellow resident the day before I went to CHOP for my first appointment. I did not share what I was expecting from the situation because I was working on my faith, but her stance was, 'I will support you whatever you decide to do'. She went with me for most of my appointments until my husband returned from Nigeria. I was glad I did not have to do this alone.

That was the second lesson I learned. Don't go through a crisis alone.

The next day, I told a colleague at work. I felt I had to because I was doing a rotation in the NICU. There was almost no way for me to be gone for appointments unnoticed. I figured if I told her, she would have my back. 'You and your husband are young, you should abort that baby', she said matter of factly. I thanked her and never spoke to her about my pregnancy again.

I learned a third lesson that day. Don't let negative people anywhere near you when you are going through a crisis.

Does that mean I was strong the entire time? No! A thousand times no! I had weekly appointments from 21 weeks and I was given the option and encouraged to have an abortion at every one of those visits until I was

24 weeks pregnant. After 24 weeks, they could no longer offer me an abortion so that was a relief, but the visits were still tough.

At one of her visits, the covering doctor told me, 'Her lungs are at 10% of the normal capacity'. At another, the ultrasound tech (who is not supposed to discuss her findings) accidentally blurted out her thoughts: 'They (referring to her doctors) really think these are lungs'?

So, no, I was not strong the entire time but what I was was a fighter all the time. Every time I felt discouraged, I went back to what the Bible said and I would get encouraged. I would call my husband and we would talk and I would get encouraged. I would not stop until the discouragement was gone.

Feeling weak on and off is fine, even normal, but you can't quit.

As I write this, I am just grateful. She will be 10 years old in less than 2 months. She truly is a miracle baby. She has been on no medication and, had no complications or long-term sequelae from all this. Our only reminder is the scar she has on her upper abdomen.

It is amazing how a short while after women have babies, they forget all they went through and get ready for another one. When Cheta was less than a year old, I was ready for another baby. I did not start having babies early and felt I had a short window. The only problem was I had so much pain from the C-section that I had made a decision that no one would cut me with a knife again. Note that the only reason I had the first C-section was that the doctors thought the baby would not be able to tolerate labor. I am not recommending that you do what I did.

I trusted God to help me and cooperated with my doctor. There were about 6 doctors in the Ob/Gyn group and only one of them, Dr. Steven Lopatine agreed that I could do a VBAC (Vaginal birth after C-section). The others were vehemently against it. This pregnancy was perfect- no morning sickness, no aches and pains and I was going to have a little boy on 12/10/2009. We were delighted.

THE FIGHT TO BECOME

I bargained with God that I would go into labor on the 3rd of December so that I would not have to go anywhere near the OR but that was not His plan. On the 9th of December, I went in for my pre-op appointment, had blood drawn and was given a tour of my pre-op room. I was still hanging on to God for dear life because I really could not imagine having another C-section. At midnight, 7 hours before he was scheduled to be born by C-section, labor started. It was hilarious when I got to the hospital and I was laboring in my pre-op room. The doctor on call, however, had no interest in delivering me so she kept me comfortable overnight and then the doctor that was to take over walked in. I was honestly amazed. It was Dr. Lopatine! The only one who was all for a VBAC. Within 30 minutes I think, I gave birth to an 8 pound healthy baby boy with no surgery!

CHAPTER SEVEN
Parenting, the most overwhelming thing I have ever done.

By 2010, I had been married for 4 years, I had an infant and a toddler, was co-pastoring a new church with my husband and we had just started Ivy League Pediatrics. The other part that I failed to mention in all this is that I also got a job at the Children's Healthcare of Atlanta (CHOA) Emergency Department and was working there anywhere from 12-20 hours per week. To say that I was busy is putting it mildly.

Now every working parent is familiar with the guilt trips we go on when we think of not being there as much as we think we should for our children. I had that but it was on overdrive.

Let me pause here to say this. If you are going to do a project, whether it is a new business, nonprofit, or ministry, you must understand that there is an opportunity cost to it. The same way joining the army changes a family dynamic, ANY project will change your family dynamic. Don't be thrown off by it, strategize to make it work.

In my case, my husband had the more flexible schedule because he could do a lot of his work remotely and I had my brother living with us.

We decided how long of a stretch of a crazy schedule I would do and they would try to make up for it. Was it perfect? No. Did it work? Yes. Are our kids ok? Yes.

Back to my crazy schedule.

Some days I would work till 3 pm at the practice, head on out to CHOA and work a 4 pm to 12 am shift. Of course, by the time I got home, the kids were asleep. I would look at my home and it did not have the homely look I wanted. There were home-cooked meals but rarely by me.

I was keenly aware of my deficiencies as a parent. It did not help that I would meet all these moms who seemed perfect. Perfect homes, kids looked perfect, they had all home cooked meals, in fact, one mom in particular made homemade gluten-free granola bars for her 2 daughters!!!

Every blog and every family movie made me even more insecure. I was sure I was breaking my kids. I was frightened that they will grow up having missed some critical training they should have gotten from me and because of that would miss out on some opportunities in the future. I thought I was a failure.

One night, I had just come back from a 4 pm-12 am shift at the Children's Hospital and I have a Eureka moment.

I suddenly became aware of these facts:

- My kids belong to God and He will ultimately take care of them.
- He needs me to do my best in raising them.
- My best means every day I strive to become a better parent. Perfection is not required, just progress.
- I am in the middle of a transition (At this time, I was an employee, a business owner, a co-pastor

of a young church, wife, and mom of 2 little children). My life is going to look a little different from others who are not doing the same things I am doing. It will be weird for a while and then everything will become more stable.

What a relief! I don't have to be perfect. I don't have to be solely responsible for how my kids turn out and a little bit of chaos for that season was fine.

Am I perfect now, 8 years later? No, nowhere near! I still don't make gluten-free granola bars! Am I much better? Yes. I am making progress every day. Do I still have to battle these guilt trips? Yes. It does not come up as often or as badly, and I know how to handle it now.

I am not perfect, but I am enjoying being a mother, I am doing my best and God is doing the rest.

This is one of the main reasons why I created the Legacy Parent Show. This is an online show that I host every Thursday on the Ivy League Pediatrics Facebook page. I partner with parents to learn more about parenting and realize that all they need is progress, not perfection.

CHAPTER EIGHT
My struggle with depression

Before I go into this, here is my disclaimer. In this chapter, I am referring to the sadness and anxiety that almost everyone who has not done a thorough work on their mindset goes through. If you have chronic depression and are on medication, this will help but please do not stop your medical plan without consulting your doctor. Also, if you feel so overwhelmed and you think you need help, get the help you need.

I was a deeply introverted child and continued that way as an adult. I don't remember being carefree and happy the way only those with a sanguine temperament can be.

This really made me feel like I was trapped. I wanted to talk to people, make friends and be genuinely happy but I just couldn't.

THE FIGHT TO BECOME

As if this was not bad enough, I had low self-esteem. Now, my parents were great and I really had a wonderful childhood. Till today, I have no idea what the root of the low self-esteem was. I constantly had these kinds of thoughts swimming around in my mind:

'I'm not good enough.'
'Other people are better than me.'
'People think I'm dumb.'
'She does not want to be my friend.'
'Other people can make good grades but I can't.'
Maybe you can identify with some of those.

A few people will be shocked when they read this and that is because I did a really good job of hiding this. No one would have thought I was an extrovert, but no one could have guessed what was going on in my mind.

In fact, I'll share a story of what happened in my first year of medical school to help you understand how bad it was. In my first year, I came into the school with the mindset that 'everyone here is better than me', and 'I don't really belong here'. What that did was it made me put forth a horribly mediocre effort. I went to class and I studied but all from the standpoint of, 'I'm not really that good, so any grade I get will be just fine as long as I don't fail outrightly'.

The weird thing about the mind is that it does not follow reason. I was an honor student in high school and I got into medical school a year earlier than most people in my class. I was historically smart but still felt like a dummy.

Anyway, I had this attitude the entire first semester and ended up with mostly Bs!! Then it hit me:
YOU BELONG HERE. YOU ARE SMART. NO ONE IS BETTER THAN YOU.
After that semester, I never had all Bs. I was mostly an A student and excelled the rest of medical school.

However, the thoughts still plagued me in most areas of my life. I would wake up on the proverbial wrong side of my bed and it will seem like the whole day would just spin the wrong way. I would be sad all day for no reason. My life was good, but I had a plethora of negative thoughts going through my head all the time. I was miserable, and I did not know what to do with it. As a result of how I thought, I believed something was seriously wrong with me.

THE FIGHT TO BECOME

Worse still, I had thoughts of disaster always on the back of my mind. As I drove to work, thoughts of getting into an accident would keep flashing. As I approached someone to talk to them, thoughts of them thinking I was a fool would keep flashing. When we started Ivy League Pediatrics, thoughts of it failing would keep flashing. It never stopped!

One day, I listened to Joyce Meyer and I am so glad I did. She is a Bible teacher who is very real and practical. She'd tell stories of how crazy her mind was. Everything aggravated her- doing the dishes, her husband going to play golf while she worked, people getting along in life and she wasn't. And I thought to myself- I am not crazy after all! She identified what the problem was- the mind. She explained that the mind is a battlefield. You don't just leave any crazy thought there to fester. She apparently had gotten so good at this battle that she had a new theme in life- ENJOYING EVERYDAY LIFE. That was what she called her show and she seemed to be living it out. That was exactly what I wanted, to enjoy everyday life.

On that day many years ago, my journey began. I am still on that journey, but boy, have I made some progress. My bed now has only one side- the right side. I probably have more 'problems' now than I did then, but they don't faze me because I have learned to fight for peace, I have learned to be calm in the face of storms, I have learned to be optimistic about life and I have learned to love myself.

So how do I fight? I'll show you the 4 simple steps.

1. I committed my life to God.

I am not sure what triggered this, but I came to the decision one day that I do not want to be the boss of my own life anymore. It was just way too much responsibility and I honestly sucked at it.

2. I changed my thoughts.

I started using a 'microscope' to examine my thought patterns and I would remove all negative thoughts and replace them with God thoughts. I am fully aware that at the end of the day you become what you think.

As a man thinketh in his heart, so is he- Solomon

If you think you can or you think you can't you are right - Henry Ford

THE FIGHT TO BECOME

If that is the case, the question becomes,
What do you think about your future?
What do you think about your health?
What do you think about your marriage? Children?
What do you think about your finances?

It is important to examine because we are all like gigantic magnets. We pull what we think about towards us.

As a person of faith, I went on a journey to find out just what God has to say about the different areas of my life because I surely did not want to see what I was thinking come to pass. These are a few of the things I came up with:

Fear not, there is nothing to fear (one of my all-time favorites)

And then I came up with a list of power confessions

I am God's masterpiece

I am destined for greatness

My life is the solution to a problem in my generation

I am different from others because I am unique

I have a prosperity mindset

I am debt-free

All my needs are met and I have plenty to spare

I am generous just like God my father

I excel at work and qualify for promotion after promotion

My business prospers

I have favor with people

I attract people who help me become the best version of me

I am in the best shape/health of my life

I am fit, firm and muscular.

I am disciplined person

THE FIGHT TO BECOME

I am experiencing abundance in every aspect of my life

You might say, well these are not facts in my life yet. I agree but neither are the scary things you think about most of the time. You think about not having enough money for retirement, losing your job, your spouse leaving you, your children not turning out right. None of these are real but it does not stop the thoughts from coming.

So just replace a negative nonfact thought with a positive "nonfact" thought.

3. I changed my words.

After I discovered some wrong thoughts and the right thoughts I found out something else. When I would go through something and get a flood of wrong thoughts, I would try to think my way out of it. Then I learned something else. You can't think the wrong thoughts away, you have to say the right words out of your mouth. Now, I am a very conservative highly intellectual person and I thought this was ridiculous at first but when I saw that I was making no progress, I gave in.

If you feel the way I felt (that it does not take all that) then I invite you to try this simple experiment.

Start counting to ten in your mind, then say your full name out loud. What you will notice is that you will have to stop counting to say it.

You can interrupt the messy thoughts in your head by saying the right thing out of your mouth.

4. I took action, no matter how I felt.

One of the things that will build your confidence like crazy is getting results. If you will take action in the direction of your goals in spite of how you feel, you will find things changing and it will boost your confidence and make you feel great about yourself.

After I had my last daughter, I gained 50 lbs and I needed to get rid of the first 40 fast. I did not like the way I looked with all that extra weight. I wasn't morbidly obese or anything of the sort, but I felt the need to fix it fast. I hated running (just not my preferred method of exercise), but I started running in spite of the feeling. I even did a 5k walk/run. I did not feel like it but when I found myself 40 lbs lighter in 4 months, I felt like a million bucks.

Don't let your feelings of anxiety or depression or sadness stop you from doing. Getting results is part of your therapy.

Today, people wonder how I am able to cope so well under pressure, how I am consistently cheerful, and it is from years of doing just what I told you.

You can use my list of power confessions to start as you take your time to make a customized list. If you start doing this, you can truly get rid of the misery and the silent cry for help that no one hears. You can go from having to pretend everything is alright to actually being alright, and like Joyce Meyer says, enjoying everyday life!

CHAPTER NINE
My power habits

Habits are little things that bring big results. We all have them. The question is if they are good or bad. The only habits you can develop by default, for the most part, are bad habits, just like weeds growing in a garden by default. You will have to be deliberate about forming the right ones.

Over the years, I have developed some habits that have served me well. I will love to share these with you. If you don't have these habits, you should start developing them. When you start, you will stumble so don't let that make you stop. Don't quit. When you stumble, pick yourself up and keep going. Just remember that when a one-year-old takes his first step and then falls, everyone celebrates. No one is disappointed. He gets up and then does it again. Do the same. Don't be disappointed, get up and do it again.

THE FIGHT TO BECOME

1. Reading- You will be the same person in five years as you are today except for the people you meet and the books you read - Charlie "Tremendous" Jones.

Reading has been one of the things that has transformed my life. I got a great education but there are so many things that I did not learn at school. Through the habit of reading, I learned how to:

- Be a great wife
- Raise my kids
- Manage money
- Start a business
- Build a team
- Be a people person
- Set and achieve goals

The list is endless. Initially, I read 12 nonfiction books a year and then I kept upping my game until I got to 50 books a year.

If you will read even a book a month and make 3-5 changes based on each book, that will be 36-60 changes per year. Your life will not be the same.

It was Jim Rohn who said:

Formal education will make you a living; self-education will make you a fortune.

You must develop this habit.

2. Building my network- Some people have poor social networks because they are very introverted, others because they don't think they need people. I was the former, but both sides are terribly wrong. Your social network is your social capital. It is as powerful as money. There are things in life that money cannot get you, but the right contact can. I have been deliberate about building my networks and not just one group of people but the 3 major ones: Mentors, colleagues, and mentees.

- Mentors:

    Your mentor in 30 minutes can unravel a problem that you have been dealing with for over 5 years. I know that people say there is no shortcut to success, but the truth of the matter is that your mentors are your shortcut. Seek out those who are where you are trying to go. Don't wait for mentors to find you, they will not. Don't be afraid to pay for mentorship or to travel to meet with someone who has agreed to give you their time.

I remember a practice I had watched from afar that was doing a lot of the things I dreamt of doing at Ivy League Pediatrics and doing them very well. I summoned up courage and sent the owner an email asking if I could come watch her practice in operation. To my shock and delight, she said yes! I bought my ticket from Atlanta to Houston, stayed in a hotel for the night and showed up in her office on time even before the staff got there. She was so gracious and let me learn from her all day. That meeting cost me money but has saved me at least 10 times what it cost me in the last 6 months alone. Don't try to go through life without mentors. You need mentors!

Now, they should be 20 steps ahead of you, not 200. For example, if the most you have made in one year is $30,000, a billionaire is not the business coach you need. Someone making $120,000- $1 million may be better. A billionaire's financial strategies may make no sense to you until you cross into a net worth of over $1 million dollars.

- Colleagues:

    Life is an uphill task, it is just the way it is. We are designed to overcome the challenges, and having a group of people fighting through obstacles will make your journey so much easier. Your colleagues are those on the same level with you, who are striving like you are. They are the ones you can run to when things don't seem to be going your way or when you are overwhelmed, because that will happen. After my early years, I decided that rather than spend 5 days trying overcome the overwhelm, I will go to my colleagues and overcome it in 30 minutes.

- Mentees:

    Those that I mentor inspire me to keep going like I cannot explain. Your life is too small to be the only reason why you are alive. Imagine at your 85th birthday party, your family stands up to talk about you (which is usual) but after that 5, 12, 50 or even 72 people unrelated to you step forward to say their piece. They talk about how their lives were headed nowhere fast until they met you. How you inspired them and held them accountable until they became successful. Imagine that.

You may say, 'How can I help anyone while my life is such a mess?' You don't need to be perfect to be a mentor, you just need to be a little further ahead. If all you have done is learned to read, help someone else become a reader. If you have developed a strong work ethic, help someone else do the same. If you have learned to keep a clean home, help someone else. If you got out of debt, please help someone else do the same. Do you see it? You don't have to be perfect. Just teach someone else what you have learned and are practicing.

3. Automobile university- This is the college of the ultra-successful. The average American's commute to work is 26 minutes. That is 52 minutes a day, 260 minutes a week, 17 hours a month and an unbelievable 204 hours a year. 204 hours in the car. Rather than listen to music, the news, or idly chatting on the phone, use this time to listen to audio programs, audio books and other motivational messages that will transform your life. If you will do this, your life will change

by leaps and bounds. In fact, if you will only do it half the time- for example, your commute to work, that will give you 102 hours of content. You can learn how to uplevel your business, build a better relationship with your teenage son, get out of debt and become a better leader, all in the time you already spend going to work.

4. Giving- I have a funny saying that I tell my husband often. I don't know why people say you cannot buy happiness. You absolutely can if you will learn to be a giver. Life is designed more for output than input. If someone gives you a brand new house, you might be beside yourself with excitement but if you give someone a brand new house, you will be on a high for a while. Be a giver. Be generous. Set giving goals, and every year, plan to surpass your giving from the previous year.

5. Review goals- Out of sight is out of mind. After you have developed the discipline of setting goals, you have to keep it at the forefront of your mind. One of the habits I have had over the years is that I review my goals daily. I actually read them out loud. It is this habit that created in me

a pipeline flowing with ideas of things I could do that would move me in the direction of my goals. Prior to developing these habits, I would set goals in the first week of January only to wonder what they were in December. No wonder I made little progress. This habit is truly a game changer. You can hang your goals in your bathroom where you will always see them, or in your daily planner or taped on your desk. Do whatever you must, but keep them in front of you.

6. Date night- My marriage is very important to me and it is not something I would like to lose because I was chasing a career. A few years ago, after listening to another couple we respect who have mentored us, we scheduled a date night. This is an evening where we spent time together, catch up on what is going on with each other, have fun, laugh and relax. It is known to be a non-negotiable event, even our kids have this puzzled look on their faces if it is Tuesday evening and we are home. Marriages, like cars, need maintenance. Don't neglect yours.

7. Time with God- This is the granddaddy of all my habits. Life is full of uncertainties and

disappointments, ups and downs, trials and pains, and I don't have what it takes to fix all that or to even understand what is really going on. It is beautiful to hand all that over to God and then do what I believe He is leading me to. I start off my day spending time with him and reading my Bible. When I pray, I commit the day into His hands because this is what He says:

Commit your actions to the LORD, and your plans will succeed. (Proverbs 16:3)

When I read my Bible, I learn solid principles of success. You know, for the last three years, I have read no less than 50 books a year. It never ceases to amaze me that most of the business principles that the greats teach are also found in the bible. The other thing that happens when I read the Bible is that I see myself for who God has told me I am.

I may feel like a failure, but He says I am more than a conqueror.

I may be told that I am no good, but He says I am the apple of His eyes.

I may be afraid, but His word says He is with me, so I don't have to be afraid.

THE FIGHT TO BECOME

This habit is the reason why I can keep my calm in the midst of the storm, why I hold on when I feel like nothing is working and why I can be hopeful that it is all going to be alright.

CHAPTER TEN
My most powerful life lesson

I have learned a ton of lessons in my 39 years. However, there is one that has stood out. You see, like many people, I thought I did not have control over my life. I thought things, whether good or bad just randomly happened to me.

2 years ago, I had a Eureka moment. It dawned on me:

I AM THE CENTER OF GRAVITY OF MY LIFE. IF I CHANGE, EVERYTHING WILL CHANGE.

I had always thought my life was subject to chance, but it was not really.

I cannot control the weather or the stock market or the government but there is one thing under my control and that is me. If I will discipline myself and consistently uplevel myself, my life will continue to get better and better. Let me unpack this so you will get it.

If I become a better spouse, my marriage will be better.

If I become a better boss, my staff will be more productive.

If I become better at managing money, there will be less financial pressure in my life.

If I become better at wealth creation, I will have more money.

If I become a nicer person, more people will want to be my friend.

If I acquire more skills as an entrepreneur, my company will break new revenue records.

The recurring thread in this is ME.

One of my main jobs in life is to make me better. If I will focus on that instead of complaining or wishing things were better, things will constantly get better.

This lesson is so liberating because it moves me from the victim line to the control line. If I want to see changes, I just go to work on me.

This is why it is a crime not to be a reader, not to have a coach and not to invest in audio programs and audio books. If you do not work on you, your life will never change.

The sad part is that if you are not actively getting better, you are getting worse. Why? Because those around you are getting better.

For example, Blockbuster stayed the same while Netflix was getting better. Blockbuster was not really staying the same. By refusing to change, they were getting worse and they finally went out of business.

Strive to get better each day. Learn new things deliberately and do new things.

There are a lot of things I do now that I knew nothing about, but I have had to constantly reinvent me. In 2005, I was not a wife or mother or pastor or business owner or professional speaker or author. I had to develop myself in all these areas and I am still doing that aggressively even today.

It is time to stop the blame game.
It is time to stop wishing things were better.

THE FIGHT TO BECOME

It is time to stop rolling over and playing dead because the problems will not go away.

If you will take the time to start working on your real project- YOU- everything will change for you.

Here's to a brand new you!

CHAPTER ELEVEN
My Superpower

Sometimes I think about my journey so far and I am just amazed at what God has done. I look back at the many times I've had to reinvent myself, at the many times I did things I thought I'd never do and the challenges I've overcome. One day, I came to the realization that I didn't go through any of these experiences for my own benefit.

My mentor and husband Steve always says, 'Your life is too small to be the only reason you exist.' Truer words have never been spoken! Imagine if all we do with our lives is grow up, go to college, get a good job, get married, have 2.5 kids and retire. What? There's got to be more!!!! Thank God.......there is.

The good news is, you don't have to look far for the "more". The more is in the lessons you've learned along the way. The more is in the positive changes you can bring to the world-one person at a time. The more is in the legacy you leave behind. You may be saying, 'what do I have to give?' My answer to you is 'much more than you think!'

No matter where you are now in your life, there is someone you can teach! There are things you've learned to do that someone else is struggling with. Forget how small or insignificant you think your skills are, there is someone out there that can learn from you. That person's life can be so changed that it will impact the generations after them.

There are people in need waiting on the other side of your obedience.

Think about the impact of encouraging someone to go to college who comes from a family that no one ever has? It will take a little effort on your part but imagine if they do go. Imagine the ripple effect it will have on their financial status, their future children, their lives! It cannot be measured. Not only that, how likely are they to 'pay it forward' to encourage their family and friends to go? Very likely. And you would be responsible for changing the social and financial status of someone's entire lineage by one act of selflessness!

Still not convinced? Ask yourself these questions:
- What is one thing that I'm good at?
- What is something I love to talk about?
- What have I done that I'm proud of?
- What have others told me they admire about me?
- What do I do easily?
- What do I wish someone had told me when I was younger?
- What problem do I feel passionate about fixing?

Found what you have to offer yet? Once you do, start teaching that thing to someone else. Investing in others is messy but so worth it! It takes time out of your schedule, sometimes they aren't appreciative (to say the least), and you may not see results right away. Take it from me though, your accomplishments mean so much more when you help others achieve along the way.

I never thought of myself as much of a mentor. When my husband and I started Dominion City Church in Georgia, I saw myself as just his helper. You can imagine the fear that gripped my heart when he told me 'you know you are the one that will mentor the women' in his usual matter-of-fact way. 'Well, you are the pastor, *not me*, I am just here to help', I protested internally. This was not a decision I had much say in. There were lives and destinies at stake, after all.

So, the journey began. We started with weekly women's meetings and I mentored the women the best way I knew how. I was still struggling with my own challenges as a wife, mother and business owner but I taught them what I knew! Eventually, we grew to having monthly women's conferences and I'm grateful to God that 9 years later thousands of women's lives have been impacted by those meetings.

Do you know the most ironic thing about mentorship? The mentor is the one that experiences the most growth in the process! Believe it or not, there is a level of growth you will not attain to until you start investing in others. Every parent will understand this because there is massive growth that happens inside of you as soon as that little baby for whom you are responsible comes into the world. There is growth that only happens when you take responsibility for another life.

No matter how hard you try you can't learn patience, communication skills or counseling techniques in isolation. As I poured myself into the women, I grew and became better. At first, I felt as if I'd been thrown off a cliff and I flapped wildly trying to stay afloat. Over time, with the growth that comes from consistent effort, I eventually learned how to soar effortlessly and bring others along for the ride.

Here's the icing on the cake: Each woman whose life was changed represents a nation that was changed for the better. If you change a man, you change his family, his community and eventually his nation.

Don't believe me?

Think of the people that mentored Oprah Winfrey (Maya Angelou), Mark Zuckerberg (Steve Jobs), Dr. Martin Luther King (Dr. Benjamin Mays) and Bill Gates (Warren Buffet). Wouldn't you say those mentors impacted nations through their mentees?

You never know who your child, your employee or someone seeking your help will become. Invest your best in them and let the adventure begin.

The benefits of mentoring are endless, but I'll only discuss one more. **Mentoring shows you a clearer picture of who you are and opens doors to other opportunities.** Let me explain:

I started off mentoring the women in our church individually, then as a group, and eventually hosted women's conferences, but it didn't stop there. Those experiences showed me a clearer picture of myself. I discovered that I am a natural encourager and a personal development expert. If you pinch me at 2 am, I will talk about personal development. If you ask me my favorite ice cream flavor *somehow* the conversation will get back to personal development. I discovered my superpower.

So now, I am a mentor to men and women in every sphere of life. I am a consultant to business owners, physicians, parents and CEO's to name a few. I am an author, I've hosted superb personal development conferences and created an effective online goal-setting course. All of this started with mentoring one person.

I began this book telling you about how I'm looking forward to my 40th birthday. Part of the reason why is that on that day some of the people who will join in the celebration are the lives that I impacted. Some of their stories are in the next few pages. My life has proven to be bigger than myself and I wouldn't have it any other way.

Dr. Una as a brand consultant and business mentor

I have always wanted a mentor and I've made contact with various people in the past asking for mentorship. None of it ever came to fruition, but a particular day changed this for me. I agreed to meet Dr. Una on a social basis.

Our discussion quickly changed to coaching. She wanted to know what I was doing and my long-term plans. She soaked up my anxiety like it was nothing. This is how my wonderful mentoring began with Dr. Una. She gave me little goals and steps to take. She made me accountable. She is firm and supportive. She knows her stuff.

THE FIGHT TO BECOME

The first coaching conversation with Dr. Una changed my business life! She is the real deal!

- Dr. Yinka Dosunmu, Aesthetic doctor U.K

Dr. Una has excellent business acumen and insight. Wise beyond her years, she has helped to guide me in my practice and given me sage advice. Though she is younger than me, she has a motherly touch that is firm yet loving. She is a blessing and elevates those around her! Thank you for your mentorship, Dr. Una

- Dr. T, Pediatrician, GA

Dr. Una as a CEO coach

I am the CEO of a non-profit corporation and was having serious staffing issues. Not only was the atmosphere tense in the office I was completely exasperated!!

I finally opened up to Dr. Una about my challenges and it was the most amazing thing I've ever experienced. She was *immediately* able to unravel and give a solution to the thing that had given me sleepless nights for months! All my stress, my anxiety and HR dilemmas were laid to rest in 2 minutes flat. She gave me some tips, encouraged me and held me accountable for the next steps. Now every time I have an issue she is my go-to person first.

I have been so impressed with the coaching I've received from Dr. Una that I make sure to sign up for any private or corporate coaching group she is leading. Her knowledge base is expansive, and the best part is that I know she is speaking from experience being a successful CEO herself. It's like having someone in your corner, there's no better feeling than that!

- M. Opoku-Mensah

CHAPTER TWELVE
My Why

'What is your why?' has become a popular question in our day. It is not a fad, it is something that you should know because when the storms come, when things don't seem to work out, there has to be something that helps you keep going. What is your why?

Money and things will never make you happy. You may think they will until you get them and then you realize how empty they are. The only way to truly enjoy things is to use them as they are meant to be used. They are tools. Tools you should use primarily to fulfill your why, and then also for your enjoyment.

Jesus is at the center of everything I am, everything I have and everything I've done or will ever do.

I could show you all the principles and the wisdom I have used to build the life that I have, but that is not the foundation that had held me up.

Jesus is my core. He is my best friend, my master, and He is the one who has radically transformed my life.

You might say, 'Ugh! I hate religion!' Well, that makes 2 of us. I hate religion too. That is an ugly list of dos and don'ts with no life in it.

I am an intellectual. I thought that God was for people who could not pull themselves together. As for me, 'I am all together', I told myself. Even as I type this, it sounds more ridiculous than it ever has because whoever created the human body, the earth, and all the galaxies is a whole lot smarter than me, and I need Him.

I am not talking about religion but a relationship with Jesus.

So, let me share my faith story.

I don't really remember a time when I did not have a God-awareness. I was always aware of His Presence. Whether I walked in His ways or not is another conversation altogether. Well, now that I look back, I think there are reasons why I always felt He was with me.

- My mom is a praying woman. We did not go to church when I was a child but she knew to always keep us covered in prayer. She would pray that God's hand would always be on our lives and that we would live for His glory.
- My mom could not get pregnant for more than a year after she was married (which was a complete no-no for a young Nigerian bride), and she promised God that her first child (me) would belong to Him.
- My paternal grandmother helped build the first Catholic Church in her village. She walked for miles carrying concrete to the site. I seriously doubt that God forgets things like that.

Looking at that, I don't think I stood a chance.

I guess I always felt like God was with me because He was.

That did not mean I decided to follow Him right away. I didn't. I did, however, like that I had someone to always talk to, confide in, and I never felt alone.

In my final year in medical school, I finally decided to follow Him, and everything got so much better.

It is not magic, so I did not make that decision and live happily ever after. It was a process.

The more time I spent talking with Him (aka prayer) and the more time I spent reading the Bible to learn about Him, the more my life changed. Changed how? These kinds of changes:

- I learned to live a peaceful life. No matter how much turbulence is around me, I am able to maintain my cool.
- I knew I was never alone, so the battles of life became easier to deal with.
- I became a visionary. I became able to see a preferred future and the steps I needed to take to get there.
- I overcame depression!! I used to be one of the moodiest people on the planet, but now that is a very distant memory.

My list of changes goes on and on and on!

I'd like to invite you on a journey.

It is true that there are people who have attained a level of success 'without' God, but the truth is that real success is becoming everything God created you to be, and you cannot do that without Him.

Think about yourself as a brand new phone. You can never use a phone to its full potential if you do not stay connected with the manufacturer. You will have to read the manufacturer's manual to even know what the phone is capable of. It is possible to be so ignorant of what the phone can do that you use it as a door stopper. Will it be a good door stopper, yes! Is it using up to 10% of its potential by being a door stopper, no!

Our manufacturer is God, His manual is the Bible and we thrive when we have a loving relationship with Him.

My life is a testimony of how amazing our God truly is.

I invite you to start a journey with Him. To start, all you have to do is accept Jesus as your Lord and savior and it all begins.

Say this simple prayer.

DEAR GOD IN HEAVEN, I COME TO YOU IN THE NAME OF JESUS TO RECEIVE SALVATION AND ETERNAL LIFE. I BELIEVE THAT JESUS IS YOUR SON. I BELIEVE THAT HE DIED ON THE CROSS FOR MY SINS AND THAT YOU RAISED HIM FROM THE DEAD. I RECEIVE JESUS NOW INTO MY HEART AND MAKE HIM THE LORD OF MY LIFE. JESUS, COME INTO MY HEART. I WELCOME YOU AS MY LORD AND SAVIOR.

FATHER, I BELIEVE YOUR WORD SAYS THAT I AM NOW SAVED. I CONFESS WITH MY MOUTH THAT I AM SAVED AND BORN AGAIN. I AM NOW A CHILD OF GOD.

If you prayed this prayer, please send me an email at druna@drunaacademy.com. I'd like to send you some resources to jump-start you on your journey!

Welcome to the family!!!!!! Let the fun begin.

EPILOGUE

Why did I write this story?

What do I hope will happen after you read my story?

I hope you will realize that no one is better than you.

I hope you realize that your past is just that. It is past and it's time to move on.

I hope you realize that obstacles are not problems. Like lifting weights, they may make your arms hurt but they will ultimately make them better.

I hope you realize that not knowing enough and not having money are not enough to stop you from becoming all you can be.

I hope you realize that it will take an incredible amount of action to make progress but you can do it.

I hope you realize that you can truly enjoy your life.

I hope you've figured out that if that's how Dr. Una did it, then you can do it too.

I hope you realize God made you for great things, and He is always there to help.

If you stopped dreaming because you tried so many times and failed, dream again.

If you have been dreaming but have been too scared to act, start acting.

You are only going to live this life once, make it legendary, leave a legacy!

THE FIGHT TO BECOME

WHO IS DR. UNA?

Fun facts about Dr. Una

- She hates shopping. If she is wearing anything that is not a pair of jeans or a T-shirt, her husband or her sister bought it for her.
- She got married in her dad's living room on a Tuesday.
- She loves the beach more than most things, but she can't swim.
- She doesn't know how to whistle.
- She had her first manicure at the age of 38 years.
- She learned how to drive at the age of 26 years.

The many hats of Dr. Una

- Steve's wife for 11 years.
- Mother of 4 children.
- Pastor at Dominion City Church, Norcross GA.
- CEO and Lead Pediatrician at Ivy League Pediatrics.

- Founder of Dr. Una Academy- Platform for personal and business development.
- Founder of Now You Can Girls and Now You Can Boys- an 8-week personal development course for elementary and middle school children.
- Founder of Momentum coaching- A small close-knit yearlong coaching network.
- Host for the Legacy Parent Show, an online parenting course.
- Professional speaker.

HOW CAN I WORK WITH DR. UNA?

Personal coaching network

Business coaching network

Employee training package

Business Leadership training for small businesses

Online course- Power goal setting course

Book Dr. Una to speak at your event

For more information, contact Dr. Una's team at druna@drunaacademy.com

Made in the USA
Columbia, SC
20 December 2024